FORECLOSURE AUCTIONS IN CONNECTICUT

FORECLOSURE AUCTIONS IN
CONNECTICUT

A PARALEGAL'S PERSPECTIVE

Sonya Y. Green

Palmetto Publishing Group
Charleston, SC

Foreclosure Auctions in Connecticut
Copyright © 2020 by Sonya Y. Green
All rights reserved

No portion of this book may be reproduced, stored in a retrieval system, or transmitted in any form by any means–electronic, mechanical, photocopy, recording, or other except for brief quotations in printed reviews, without prior permission of the author.

The information provided in this book does not and is not intended to constitute legal advice. Instead, all information, content, and material available in this book are for general informational use only. This information may not constitute the most up-to-date information. The book contains references to links to websites. Such website references are only for the convenience of the reader, user, and/or browser. No reader of this book should act or refrain from acting on the basis of the information in this book without first seeking legal advice from counsel in the relevant jurisdiction. Only your individual attorney can provide assurances that the information contained herein and your interpretation of it is applicable or appropriate to your particular situation. Use of and access to this book or any of the resources contained within the book do not create an attorney-client relationship between the reader, user, and/or browser.

These website links are public records, which are not guaranteed to accurately reflect the information contained therein. The views expressed in or through this book are those of the individual author writing in her individual capacity as a paralegal only, not those of an attorney at law. All liability with respect to actions taken or not taken based on the contents of this book is hereby expressly disclaimed. The content is provided "as is," and no representations are made that the content is error-free.

First Edition

Printed in the United States

ISBN-13: 978-1-64111-736-4
ISBN-10: 1-64111-736-2

CONTENTS

Introduction	vii
Chapter 1: General Information regarding Foreclosures	1
General Information regarding Auction/Sale Process	2
Truths about Foreclosure Auction Properties	4
Chapter 2: Types of Foreclosures	6
Chapter 3: Recognizing the Best Buy for Your Money	9
Chapter 4: Researching Foreclosure Auction Properties That You Are Interested in Purchasing	10
Where to Locate Foreclosure Auction Properties	10
What You Need to Know about the Property and Where to Find It	12
Liens That Survive the Foreclosure Auction	32
Blight Liens	33
Attend Auction	35
Close with Court-Appointed Committee	36
What to Do after Title Passes/Problems That May Arise	36
Exceptions to a Successful Foreclosure Auction Sale/Reasons Why Sale Is Canceled	37
Bonus	37
Chapter 5: Municipal Tax Deed Sales	38

INTRODUCTION

FOR WHOM DID I WRITE THIS BOOK?

I write this book for all persons interested in purchasing foreclosure auction properties. I have found in recent years that there has been lots of interest in foreclosure auction properties. Lots of contractors, business owners, and investment professionals have been invading the market to generate additional income. For whatever reason someone wants to purchase foreclosure auction properties, this book is here to provide useful information to facilitate the transaction. Also, it will allow you to have guidance in one single resource that directs you to the proper websites to assist with the many details one looks for when committing to the purchase of foreclosure auction properties.

WHY WRITE THIS BOOK?

I am writing this book in hopes of sharing my knowledge gained about how to purchase a foreclosure auction property successfully within the state of Connecticut. It's not enough just to have the money to buy at the sale. You need to do your own research about the property and/or properties you are interested in buying. The court appoints an attorney to sell the property, but you cannot rely solely on what information he or she may have. As an interested buyer, you need to do your own due diligence in finding out everything there is to know about the foreclosure auction property you seek to purchase.

That is where I come in. I love to help people, and over the years I have acquired unique skills from my work experience. In my experience as a foreclosure paralegal for over thirty years—specifically handling auction properties—I have discovered how to better equip people as they attempt to purchase property at foreclosure auctions. I talk to people about more than just sale details, but I also extend my wealth of information regarding how to shop for foreclosure auction properties geared toward each person's specific needs. I found that people buy for different reasons: restore and resell, rent out a house as an investment, rent it out themselves, or live in it themselves.

I believe I can help people learn as much as they can about a piece of foreclosure auction property before they can firmly commit to that sale. This book contains all the informational websites that will assist you in researching the property of interest. With all the people I have spoken with over the years, and still do today, all have said they are grateful for the information I have been able to provide. *I do not offer legal advice*, but I do provide instruction and direction as to what to look for and how to handle the information you obtain as you prepare to participate in a foreclosure auction sale.

It should be noted that this book is intended for those who are interested in learning how to buy properties at foreclosure auctions ordered by the court and not properties that are already listed by banks as foreclosure properties. All information contained herein is strictly based upon my own knowledge obtained through my experience as a paralegal in the state of Connecticut.

WHAT IS THIS BOOK ABOUT?

When purchasing foreclosure auction properties, you need to know what is important to you in your search. *Research* is the most important skill to a successful purchase. You want to prepare yourself to know everything about properties available at a foreclosure auction. You want to know the value of the property, if there are any liens on the property, the title history, where to find the property's tax and sewer information, and how the auction process works. I can help you locate this information and have it right at your fingertips. Most of this information is public, and you can obtain it quickly if you just have internet access. All you need to know is where to look.

This book will give any individual the tools he or she needs to discover specific aspects about a property prior to purchasing said property at a foreclosure auction. While these tools direct all activity toward purchasing foreclosure auction properties, they can also be used in a search to buy a regular piece of property as well, with a few exceptions.

In today's market, I see a lot of people looking to purchase foreclosure auction properties to fix and resell. It is what people used to call flipping of properties for profit. The information in this book will greatly assist those who seek to purchase foreclosure auction properties.

For those seeking to purchase foreclosure auction properties within the state of Connecticut and from out of the state of Connecticut, this book is for you! My hope, especially for those of you who are serious about investing in these foreclosure auction properties in Connecticut, is that the wealth of my knowledge shared in this book will greatly enhance your experience and make your auction property purchase easier.

For those who just want to know the "how" part, you can skip to chapter 4, which gives all the details on how and where to research.

CHAPTER 1

GENERAL INFORMATION REGARDING FORECLOSURES

For those who are unfamiliar with foreclosures, here is a bit of information to introduce you to it. A foreclosure action is a civil lawsuit brought against someone or some entity that owes a debt that is secured by real property and has not been paid for some time. The person or entity bringing the action is the **plaintiff**, who is owed the debt. The person or entity owing the debt is the **defendant**, the property owner. The property owner is usually listed as the first named defendant. All other defendants listed as parties in the action are individuals and/or entities that have an interest in the property by virtue of a lien on the property or may be another titleholder to the property.

A foreclosure can only be brought if there is a property that has been used for security or collateral against the debt. If there are other defendants that are owed money as well, they are entitled to get what they are owed from a foreclosure action in either of two ways: judgment by strict foreclosure or judgment by foreclosure sale.

If judgment enters by strict foreclosure, law days are entered, leaving the property open only to parties in the action, an opportunity to obtain title. Generally, judgment of strict foreclosure is ordered where the court has determined there is no equity in the property, based upon the ratio of the debt to the appraised value of the property. An exception would be if the IRS or any federal government entity is a party; then the court would issue a foreclosure by sale, regardless of the lack of equity, since the only way to clear title of a federal entity lien is by a foreclosure auction.

Law days are days ordered by the court in which each defendant is issued its own law day. On each law day, a specific defendant is given the option of redeeming or paying off the debt the property owner owed to the plaintiff in order to protect their interest. This is assuming that no other defendant that was issued a prior law day has done so before. If they redeem, then they obtain title to the property, and all other defendants lose their interest in the property. If no one redeems, title vests in the plaintiff, and all other defendant parties in the action lose their interest in the property. This is not what this book is about.

If judgment by sale is ordered, an auction is ordered. This is mostly because there is substantial equity in the property compared to the debt owed by the property owner, *or*, as previously mentioned, a federal entity is a party to the action. Of course, the above exception regarding federal government entity liens is applicable here as well.

Judgments ordered as foreclosure by sale are the actions yielding you your opportunity to obtain property. This is for us! These actions represent opportunities for other defendants in the action, not the property owner, to protect their interest. You and all defendants in the action stand on equal ground since all of you must bid against each other on the property at the sale.

GENERAL INFORMATION REGARDING AUCTION/SALE PROCESS

Once a sale is ordered, the process is as follows. The committee will start its work on a date ordered by the court. This is usually forty-five days prior to the sale date. Once this begins, an ad is posted on the judicial website (www.jud.ct.gov), a sign is posted on the premises, and an ad is posted in the newspaper. The newspaper is chosen by the court. In the interim, a title report and appraisal are ordered. During that time, any person interested in the property would call or email the committee regarding additional information about the property. The property owner can, at any time, prevent the auction from going forward by any means available to him, her, or it. This is unlikely but it is still a possibility. Once the committee gets a bid from the plaintiff, whether it can either be disclosed to prospective bidders or not is determined by the plaintiff. If you are really interested in a property and cannot get the bid, you will have to attend the sale to find out. On the sale date, the committee will check to make sure that all parties interested in bidding have a bank check for the deposit amount. This deposit allows you to bid on the property. It is also a good idea to make the bank check payable to yourself so that if you are not the successful bidder, you will not have a hard time getting funds back from your bank. Once the committee verifies deposits, you will sign a registration of bidders and be issued a paddle with a number. The auction will start promptly at the time ordered by the court. At that time, the committee will represent what the plaintiff's bid is, and then all other parties still interested will bid above that until a final bid is had. The final bidder becomes the successful purchaser of the property. He or she will sign a sales agreement in duplicate and endorse his or her deposit check over to the clerk of the Superior Court. One copy comes back with the committee to be submitted to court, and the other copy will go with the successful bidder. The committee submits the deposit funds to the court and files a motion to approve the sale and committee deed. There is a report on it the following week. It takes about ten business days, generally, for that motion to appear on what the court calls the short calendar. Once the motion appears on the short calendar, it will be marked ready by the committee, and then the court will take time to approve the sale. It takes approximately another couple of weeks for the approval to come through. Then the court will send out the signed committee deed to the committee, and the committee is ordered to close with the successful bidder within thirty days of the notice from court. Usually, you can close on the twenty-first day after the notice. At closing, the successful bidder (or, if he or she is represented by an attorney, his or her attorney) will be given the committee deed and conveyance tax return in exchange for the remaining balance of funds due from the successful bidder. Once that deed is recorded, the title officially is in the name of the successful bidder.

Again, it should be noted that during this whole time, the property owner can prevent the sale from being completed all the way up until the closing date. It is unlikely, but still a possibility.

TRUTHS ABOUT FORECLOSURE AUCTION PROPERTIES

TRUTH: If you own property in the state of Connecticut and use it as security or collateral in any circumstance, you run the risk of that property being saddled with a lien.

TRUTH: In the state of Connecticut, foreclosure auction properties are sold "as is."

TRUTH: In the state of Connecticut, *rarely* is there access to the interior of the property prior to the auction.

Truth: In the state of Connecticut, foreclosure auction properties, as issued by a court order, are sold by a court appointed committee, except some municipal tax sales (this will be discussed later).

Truth: In the state of Connecticut, all liens are cleared from title of property when a foreclosure auction successfully occurs, with few exceptions (see further discussion).

Truth: Owners of the property may prevent the sale from being approved between the successful purchaser and the court appointed committee, up until the closing.

Truth: If there are no other bids at the auction besides the opening bid put forth by the plaintiff, title will vest in the plaintiff.

CHAPTER 2

TYPES OF FORECLOSURES

There are many types of foreclosures: mortgage, tax lien, sewer lien, water lien, mechanic's lien, judgment lien, condominium lien, cooperative lien, and now even reverse mortgage liens. For those who are unfamiliar, here is a crash course.

A. **Mortgage foreclosure:** A lawsuit brought by a bank, financial institution, or third party/entity who loaned a property owner money based upon the value of the property he or she or entity owns.

B. **Reverse mortgage foreclosure:** A lawsuit brought by a bank or financial institution with funds issued by a federal government entity, who loaned a property owner money based upon equity in the property he or she or entity owns.

C. **Condominium foreclosure:** A lawsuit brought by a condominium association for past-due common charges, special assessments, and any other assessments against the property owner. In Connecticut, condominium associations have an automatic lien against the property to protect the interest of the association. Some condominium associations allow you to rent the property, but many do not, and require that you live in the unit you buy.

D. **Cooperative foreclosures:** I have limited understanding about these foreclosure transactions other than this: in a cooperative foreclosure, you are not buying real property right out. You are buying an interest in a corporation that owns the property that gives you exclusive use to a housing unit. On top of that, you cannot rent it out; you must live in it yourself.

E. **Mechanic's lien foreclosure:** A lawsuit brought by a person and/or entity that has completed some work for the property owner but has not been paid in full or at all. He or she liens the property. This lawsuit is preempted by some other legal action that creates the lien to be placed on the property. Once on the property, then the lienholder (person who did the work) can commence a foreclosure lawsuit. These do not often make it to a foreclosure auction but are good to know about.

F. **Judgment lien foreclosure:** A lawsuit brought by a person and/or entity that is owed money by virtue of a debt owed by the property owner. Similar to a mechanic's lien, this type of foreclosure is preempted by some other legal action that creates the lien to be placed on the property. Once on the property, then the lienholder (person who is owed the money) can bring a lawsuit. These do not often make it to a foreclosure auction but are good to know about.

G. **Municipality and utility foreclosure (tax lien, sewer lien, and water lien):** These can be grouped together for explanation. The auctions that extend from these lawsuits are where the majority of the competition appears. These are brought because someone has not paid the property taxes, sewer use charges, or water use charges. Investment-wise, auctions coming from these types of lawsuits are the best properties to look at first, as they will typically yield the least amount of money to expend since the debt is usually so low. Generally speaking, the opening bid from the plaintiff is low. However, be aware that these properties are what a lot of investors look for, so there will be much competition. Some cities and towns will combine all liens into one lawsuit, but most will bring separate actions. This totally depends on the town or city, if it has separate entities to collect those debts or all are collected by any given town or city.

H. Other sales (municipal tax deed sales—see chapter 5)
    I. Frequently asked questions:
        a. What liens are assumed or stay with the property when you become the new owner?
        b. What liens are wiped out?
        c. What liens are on the property?
        d. Is there confirmation of ownership?
        e. What taxes, sewer bills, and water bills are due and owing that you will become responsible for?
        f. What taxes, sewer bills, and water bills are included in the foreclosure action?
        g. What is the occupancy of the property?
        h. How do you get tenants and/or homeowner out after closing?
        i. If there is a federal entity lien, outside of a reverse mortgage lien but such as an IRS lien, does it get wiped out? How is it handled?
        j. What other liens appear on the title?
        k. What parties are a part of the action?

CHAPTER 3

RECOGNIZING THE BEST BUY FOR YOUR MONEY

1. Determine what kind of money you have or want to spend. No matter what research you do, you will want to know this fact so you will not be researching properties out of your price range, based upon judgment debt and appraised value.
2. Look at a picture of the property, or drive by it to take in any exterior flaws in need of repair (i.e., paint, roofing, windows). You need to factor all of this into your budget.
3. Without interior access, you want to cushion your budget with extra funds in case of the necessity of interior repairs.
4. Always stay in contact with the court-appointed committee to make sure of the availability of the property you are interested in, just in case it does not get posted quickly upon cancellation.
5. Now that you have determined your financial capabilities, you can move to streamlining the choices that suit your needs.
6. Get a head start on other prospective bidders and start your pursuit. Research is the key. Start with locating the properties.

Now that you have some basic information, let's get started!

CHAPTER 4

RESEARCHING FORECLOSURE AUCTION PROPERTIES THAT YOU ARE INTERESTED IN PURCHASING

WHERE TO LOCATE FORECLOSURE AUCTION PROPERTIES

Seek out your sources to determine where to locate and discover the availability of foreclosure auction properties.

1. **Sign on property:** This method works if you are always driving around neighborhoods and stumble across a sign on the property. However, this may not be the best way since property owners, even though the sign says not to, will remove the sign from the property as soon as it goes up.
2. **Newspaper**: This is a great place to look and locate. However, sometimes you may need to be on multiple sites to see them, and you may need to check with the committee to see if they are still available.

Most courts require that advertising be posted in the newspaper. The paper will list it as a Notice of Publication, Foreclosure Sale Public

Auction, Legal Notice Foreclosure Auction Sale, Public Auction, or Foreclosure Auction. There are numerous newspapers that publish foreclosure auction ads. Those newspapers are as follows:

The Advocate
Bethel Beacon
Branford Review
Brookfield Journal
Clinton Reporter
The Day
East Hartford Gazette
The Express
Greenwich Time
Hartford Courant
Journal Inquirer
The Litchfield County Times
The Middletown Press
The Mystic River Press
New Haven Register
Newington Town Crier
North Haven Citizen
Norwich Bulletin
Pictorial Gazette
The Record-Journal
Register Citizen
Rocky Hill Post
The ShoreLine Times
Stratford Bard
Thomaston Express
Wallingford Voice

Berlin Citizen
Bloomfield Journal
Bristol Press
The Cheshire Citizen
Connecticut Post
The Dolphin
East Haven Advertiser
The Farmington Valley Post
Hamden Chronicle
The Herald Press
Kent Good Times Dispatch
Main Street News
Milford Weekly
New Britain Herald
New Milford Times
News-Times
North Haven Post
Orange Bulletin
The Plainville Citizen
Regional Standard
Republican-American
Shelton Weekly
Southington Citizen
The Hour
The Town Times
West Hartford News

West Haven News
Wethersfield Post
Windsor Journal

The Westerly Sun
Willimantic Chronicle

If the newspaper is your preferred choice of ease, you can look at any of the above papers online via www.ct.mypublicnotices.com. Newspaper ads are posted on many different days. For those who are aggressively seeking to flip property, daily searches are recommended.

Note: *Some websites are not secure, so be wary of putting in any personal information.*

3. **Judicial website (www.jud.ct.gov):** *This is the best place to look.* All properties for sale at auction in the state of Connecticut are listed on the judicial website. They are listed by town or city. Pictures of the exterior of the property are usually on the website. If the sale is canceled, you just look at the ad, and it will be marked as canceled. If it is not canceled, then check with the committee if you feel it might be.

    Once on the site, click the Public tab and then the Sales tab to the far right; then click the town or city of interest, and then click View Full Notice on any foreclosure auction property on the Pending Foreclosures page. From this website, you can also maneuver by a few clicks to where you can obtain further details about the foreclosure action.

WHAT YOU NEED TO KNOW ABOUT THE PROPERTY AND WHERE TO FIND IT

1. **Judicial website**

    Once on the judicial website and on the Pending Foreclosures page, you can look at the details of the case by clicking on the docket number; then click Case Detail at the top left-hand corner, and this will take you to the foreclosure case that prompted this sale. Here you can see all the parties involved in the case and the status of the case. This is a good preliminary start for your research. Initially, you can determine who the parties are. This is important because this may determine how much further you will need or want to go in researching a property of interest.

If a federal entity is a defendant, then you will want to stop any further research right there—*unless* 1) you really want to this property, or 2) there is still substantial equity in the property, even with the federal lien.

If a federal entity is a plaintiff, as in the case of a reverse mortgage foreclosure, the same will apply as far as there being substantial equity in the property.

If the plaintiff is a third-party entity that has captured or bought tax liens, sewer liens, and/or water liens from a town or city, these are the auctions that can prove to be very lucrative, and you will want to do all your research on them. You may not be able to identify them, but some of those third-party plaintiff entities are as follows:

Tower Fund Services as Custodian for FIG CT13, LLC
Propel Financial I, LLC
Cazenovia Creek Funding I, LLC
Cazenovia Creek Funding II, LLC
MTAG Services LLC
MTAG Services, LLC, as Custodian for Caz Creek CT, LLC
Caz Creek II, LLC
MTAG Caz Creek CT, LLC
American Tax Funding, LLC

Benchmark Municipal Tax Services, LTD
Plymouth Park Tax Services LLC d/b/a X-spand
Connecticut Tax Liens I, LLC
VMF TL1, LLC
CT Tax Liens 2, LLC
CT Tax Liens 5, LLC
TLOA of CT, LLC
TLF National Tax Lien Trust 2017-1
TTC Investments I, LLC
Cheswold (TL) LLC
Cheswold (REO) LLC
WPCA City of Hartford
WPCA City of Bridgeport
Stamford WPCA
Greater New Haven WPCA
City of Norwich Department of Public Utilities
City of Torrington Tax Collector
Town of Torrington Collector of Revenue
City of Danbury Tax Collector
City of Bristol, a municipal organization
City of Shelton, by and through its tax collector
City of New Britain
City of Meriden
City of New Haven
City of West Haven
City of Norwich
Town of Stonington
City of Stamford
City of Middletown
City of Ansonia

Another reason to know who the parties are in the lawsuit is that it allows you to compare the parties to what you find on the land records. This is important because you want to know of any other tax liens or sewer liens that may be recorded after judgment and not a part of the foreclosure action.

Also, the amounts of the relevant lien interests, or at least estimates, are listed in the complaint as long as the action was started after e-filing commenced in the state of Connecticut, which I believe was sometime around 2006.

2. **Tax Collector of the Town/City (sometimes include sewer; check tabs at top of page)**

Validate the tax and/or sewer liens. Many city and/or town websites have been developed so that you can see what taxes and, sometimes, what sewer charges are due on any foreclosure auction property you are trying to purchase. Once on the taxing authority website, you want to see if there are any additional taxes owed or if there are third parties owning taxes that would be owed by you as the buyer at the foreclosure auction. You need to contact that third party entity for further information. Generally, the taxing authority will have a contact telephone number listed. You always want to keep a record of any other taxes owed outside of the foreclosure sale. This adds a better estimate of what money you will need to purchase that particular property.

Finding out about taxes on a property can be easy and difficult at the same time. While there is a web address that can get you tax information about a piece of property in each town or city, its access is not direct.

To obtain tax information about most properties throughout the state of Connecticut, you can put in your search engine https://

www.mytaxbill.org>inet>bill>town=_____. The line after the address is to for you to fill in the specific town or city you wish to go to for tax information. For example, for Bridgeport, Connecticut, you input https://www.mytaxbill.org>inet>bill>town=bridgeport or https://www.mytaxbill.org>inet>bill>town=fairfield. You do that for each town or city. The following is a list of towns and cities that operate from this web address.

Andover	Franklin	Norwich	West Haven
Ansonia	Glastonbury	Old Lyme	Westbrook
Ashford	Goshen	Old Saybrook	Weston
Barkhamsted	Granby	Orange	Westport
Beacon Falls	Greenwich	Oxford	Wethersfield
Berlin	Griswold	Plainfield	Willington
Bethany	Groton	Plainville	Wilton
Bethel	Guilford	Plymouth	Windham
Bloomfiel	Haddam	Pomfret	Windsor
Bolton	Hamden	Portland	Windsor Locks
Bozrah	Hampton	Preston	Wolcott
Branford	Hartford	Prospect	Woodbridge
Bridgeport	Hartland	Putnam	Woodbury
Bridgewater	Hebron	Redding	Woodstock
Bristol	Kent	Ridgefield	Canterbury
Brookfield	Killingly	Rocky Hill	Enfield
Brooklyn	Killingworth	Roxbury	Lyme
Burlington	Lebanon	Salisbury	Sprague
Canaan	Lisbon	Scotland	Voluntown
Canterbury	Litchfield	Seymour	Farmington
Canton	Madison	Shelton	North Stonington
Chaplin	Manchester	Sherman	West Hartford

Cheshire	Mansfield	Simsbury
Chester	Marlborough	Somers
Clinton	Meriden	South Windsor
Colchester	Middlebury	Southbury
Colebrook	Middletown	Southington
Columbia	Monroe	Stafford
Cornwall	Montville	Stamford
Danbury	Morris	Sterling
Deep River	Naugatuck	Stonington
Durham	New Britain	Stratford
East Granby	New Canaan	Suffield
East Haddam	New Fairfield	Thomaston
East Hampton	New Hartford	Tolland
East Hartford	New Haven	Torrington
East Haven	New London	Trumbull
East Windsor	New Milford	Vernon
Eastford	Newington	Warren
Easton	Newtown	Washington
Ellington	Norfolk	Waterbury
Essex	North Canaan	Waterford
Fairfield	North Haven	Watertown

Once you get the town or city page, then you can search for tax records by owner name or property address or bill number. The site gives you current taxes owed, past taxes paid, what amounts are delinquent, and whether any of those delinquent taxes have been sold to a third party. If that is the case, you may see a directive for someone to contact regarding those grand list years. If so, maybe you can get that information from the court-appointed committee in the matter. If not, then you need to contact that third party to find out what those past due taxes are, especially if the action is started by a separate third party action. Please be aware that sometimes, when you have a tax, sewer, or water lien foreclosure, the third party entity bringing the lawsuit may only be suing on taxes, sewer, and/or water liens it bought from the town or city, and there may still be other taxes, sewer, and/or water liens owed by other third party entities. You want to know this prior to the sale, so if you are the successful purchaser, you will not be caught by surprise with a whopping tax, sewer, and/or water bill that you did not know about. The committee may or may not acquire said information for the sale.

Note: Some websites are not secure, so be wary of putting in any personal information.

The following towns and cities have separate sites.

- Town of Darien (www.darien.gov). Go to the website. At the bottom of page, go to Additional Links. Click View/Pay Taxes. Click Agree. Search tax records by name (owner of property).
- Town of Ledyard (www.town.ledyard.ct.us). Go to the website. Click Departments. Click Tax Collector. Click Online Payments. Click "Pay taxes and sewer/water assessment bill online." Click "I agree" to the disclaimer. Search taxes by name, last name, then first name (owner of property). It will give real property, personal property, and motor vehicle taxes. You only want real property tax information; that's what you pay attention to.
- Town of Norwalk (www.norwalkct.org). Go to the website. Click "E-tax bill look up." Put in the name of the owner. Click Search. Then select the appropriate one based upon Owner and Address tabs.

- Town of Salem (www.salemct.gov). Go to the website. Click Departments. Click Tax Collector. Click the Pay Taxes Online tab. Click "I agree" to the disclaimer. Search by name (owner of property). Pay attention to real estate taxes only.
- Town of Winchester (www.townofwinchester.org). Go to the website. Click Departments. Click Tax Collector. Under "To make an online payment," click "Please pay online by clicking this link." Click "I agree" to the disclaimer. Search by name (property owner). Pay attention to real estate taxes only. While there may be multiple or similar last names, check the entries for real estate taxes only and the property address associated with it to make sure you have the right one and all the years due.

The following towns have no online access to tax records. If you find property in any of these towns, you must go to the physical tax collector's office of that town or city and inquire. Otherwise, you can rely on the committee's representation of what he or she has obtained as owed for taxes on the property. However, another alternative can be the judicial website (www.jud.ct.gov). *See chapter 4B1 on how to maneuver to the case.* There you can look at the case, review the complaint in the action to see whether there are any listed tax liens, or view the appraisal report closely to see whether the appraiser listed what the current taxes are for said property.

Unfortunately, with exception of Union, the following towns and cities usually have foreclosure auctions posted on the judicial website but have no public tax information available.

Sharon

Thompson

Union

Wallingford

Note: Some websites are not secure, so be wary of putting in any personal information.

3. **Assessor's Website**

    This website contains information regarding property as it pertains to owner, assessment of the property, value of property, and sometimes a picture of the property. Please be aware that some information may not be available or may only be up to date to a certain extent, but for the most part, it will meet your needs. Also, these sites are helpful for determining what properties are held by a city or town. It is also helpful if you are really trying to branch out and even try to buy property directly from the city or town, assuming it is available for sale.

    It is also helpful for comparing and confirming the property title owner, assuming the site is up to date with its information. Each town or city will indicate how often the site is updated (i.e., weekly, daily, monthly, bimonthly). Please also be aware that these sites are always changing. As of the writing of this book, assessor's websites were recently changed and are reflected herein.

    Getting the value of the property is sometimes a little difficult. You can rely on the appraisal done by the plaintiff in the foreclosure action. You can also rely on the committee's appraisal submitted to the court ten days prior to the sale date that has an appraised value good for ninety days. This can be obtained by visiting the judicial website, as aforementioned. Unless you are someone who has pockets burning with a lot of money, you will want to know the value of the property as soon as possible prior to the auction.

    However, if either of those methods prove fruitless, you can get an idea of the property value by visiting the assessor's website for each town or city. For a somewhat easier task for this information, you can view www.vgsi.com. It represents a lot of states, but for purposes of this book, you only need to look at Connecticut. Once there, you click the Taxpayer Info tab, then click the Assessor's Online Database tab. Then click Connecticut, and then choose the town or city of interest. This site has many towns and cities right at your fingertips for viewing. It offers you information regarding the current and past title holders, the dimensions of the property, assessed value, appraised value, and sometimes a picture of the property. You will need to know the property address for some towns or cities, or the owner name for others, or on some, you can look it up by both. The site is updated on a regular basis. However, as you will see, the regularity is daily, weekly, monthly, and so forth, depending on the town or city. Also, please be aware that some towns and cities have been deleted from the assessor's website just in the interim of gathering the information for this book. If that happens when you are looking for a certain foreclosure property in a certain town or city, you might want to visit the town or city website to see if it has established its own assessor's page for you to visit. As of now, the following are a list of the towns and cities that are currently on the above assessor's website.

Andover
Bolton
Bridgeport
Bristol
Brooklyn
Canterbury
Colebrook

Ashford
Branford
Bridgewater
Brookfield
Canaan
Clinton
Columbia

Danbury	Deep River
Eastford	East Granby
East Haddam	East Lyme
Ellington	Enfield
Essex	Fairfield
Granby	Haddam
Hamden	Hampton
Kent	Lebanon
Litchfield	Lisbon
Madison	Manchester
Middlebury	Middlefield
Middletown	Milford
Monroe	New Britain
New Fairfield	New Haven
New London	New Milford
Newtown	North Branford
North Haven	Norwalk
Norwich	Old Lyme
Old Saybrook	Orange
Oxford	Plainfield
Pomfret	Preston
Redding	Salem
Scotland	Sharon
Somers	South Windsor
Southbury	Southington
Sprague	Stafford
Stamford	Suffield
Thompson	Tolland
Trumbull	Union
Voluntown	Waterford

Westbrook	West Hartford
Westport	Willington
Wilton	Winchester
Wolcott	Woodbridge
Woodstock	

You might say, Why do I need a title search when you have all the information here? This would be true if that was all you needed. It is suggested that you do your own title research because you want to know about all liens on the property—all recorded liens, that is (any unrecorded liens other than IRS, or liens recorded after judgment was ordered). By knowing this, you can determine what you might or might not be up against after the sale—if, for example, there are additional tax, sewer, or water liens that you, as the successful purchaser, would be responsible for, as this sometimes happens after judgment enters in a foreclosure but before the auction occurs. Let's move on to title.

Note: Some websites are not secure, so be wary of putting in any personal information.

4. **Land records online (preliminary title search)**
   Other liens on property (i.e., blight liens, life use claim on property)
   Completing title research can be somewhat time consuming, especially if you are researching multiple pieces of property that may not all be in the same town. What I have discovered is that many towns and cities have moved to corporate companies that service land records searched online. Here is a listing of the main websites that maintain access to multiple towns

and cities regarding the title history.

US Land Records (Once there, click State, then Town/City.)
https://www.uslandrecords.com

Barhamsted	Hampton	Portland
Bethlehem	Hebron	Seymour
Bloomfield	Lisbon	Southbury
Bridgeport	Litchfield	Deep River
Brooklyn	Madison	Tolland
Cromwell	Deep River	Waterford
East Haddam	Middlebury	Watertown
Monroe	East Haven	Naugatuck
Woodbridge	East Lyme	Deep River

Info Quick Solutions Inc. (Once there click Town; log in as guest.)
www.searchiqs.com

Coventry	Plainfield	West Haven
Durham	Redding	Westbrook
Fairfield	Salisbury	Windham
Hartford	Sharon	Windsor
Kent	Stratford	Woodbury
Killingly	Torrington	Woodstock
New Haven	Warren	Canterbury
Norfolk	Waterbury	Colchester
Cheshire	Orange	Thompson

Kofile Technologies
https://countyfusion7.kofiletech.us

New London	East Hartford	Hebron
Putnam	Goshen	N. Stonington

Sterling Greenwich Roxbury
Washington

Town Clerk's Portal
https://connecticut-townclerks-records.com

New Britain New Canaan
Groton Newington
Killingworth South Windsor
Middletown Weston
Milford

Record Hub
https://recordhub.cottsystems.com

Ansonia Guilford Somers
Ashford Hartland Southington
Avon Harwinton Stafford
Bethany Lebanon Stonington
Bethel Manchester Suffield
Bolton Mansfield Thomaston
Bozrah Marlborough Union
Branford Montville Westport
Bridgewater Morris Willington
Burlington New Hartford Wilton
Canaan New Milford Winchester
Canton Newtown Windsor Locks
Chaplin North Branford Wolcott (index data only)
Chester North Canaan
Clinton North Haven
Colchester Old Lyme
Columbia Old Saybrook

Essex	Berlin
East Granby	Oxford
East Hampton	Plainville
Eastford	Plymouth (index data only)
Ellington	Pomfret
Farmington	Redding
Granby	Rocky Hill
Griswold	Simsbury

Once you reach one of these sites, it directs you how to look for a piece of property. Each of the sites shows information differently.

On the US land records website, click State, then Town. Once there, you need to know the first and last name of the property owner and the address of the property you are interested in (info from judicial website case detail). Once you put that name in, it may give you several to choose from, and if so, it's best to look at each one. Once you click each name, you will see what kinds of liens are on the property.

On the Info Quick Solutions website, you will be directed to the page that lists all the towns and cities in the state you are looking for that use its service. You click a town or city; then it goes to a page where you can just click "Log in as guest." Then, again, you need the first and last name of the owner. Then it brings you to a page of all liens in that town or city with that name. You can distinguish by looking to the far-right column, entitled Description, where it will let you know what property each lien is related or attached to. Those are the only liens you would really need to pay attention to for the purposes of the foreclosure property you are looking to buy. If you want to see the actual recorded documents, just click on the recorded documents in the far-left column. Sometimes, you may be able to see it without having to pay.

On the County Fusion website, you will see a host of states with the towns and cities that use their site. As you will see, in Connecticut, there are very few towns and cities that use this site. I found this site a little bit different to maneuver. You are directed to another page, where you can log in as guest. Once there, you plug in name of owner, last name, first name, or company name; then click Search at the top right of the page that reads Search. It will bring you to a listing of title owners in that town with that name.

On the Town Clerk's Portal website, changes have been made. There are only a few towns and cities where you can access land records here. This is a recent change. For those specific towns, you can log in as a guest. Click the town you are interested in (it should be only the ones listed previously, as the other towns indicate only dog license searches are available). Then search by the name of owner of the property.

As a part of the above website's changes, they have created a new site for other towns and cities that used to belong. This is the record hub website. At first visit, the site looks as if you need to pay in order to research property on the land records. However, please be patient. Once you set up an account, you can choose the complimentary plan. This allows you to input the owner's name and see what liens are attached to the property. You must pay close attention to what items belong to the property of interest. The property is listed to the far-right column.

There are still some towns and cities that have not gone corporate yet or have associated with a different type of website for land record searches. The following are towns and cities that are only accessible to the public for land record searches by virtue of paid subscriptions. If you really want auction properties in these towns, some are still free, but most require you to expend substantial moneys to do so.

Free:
- Town of Middlefield (www.middlefieldct.org). Go to the website. Once there, click the Town Offices tab. Then click the Town Clerk tab to the left. Then click, in the middle of the page, "Town of Middlefield's Land Records Search." It brings you to a disclaimer page. Choose the "Non-window user" search. On the next page, click Public Search. On the next page, accept the disclaimer. Then you are at the page that allows you to search the land records via property owner name.
- Town of Enfield (www.enfield-ct.gov). Go to the website. Once there, click the Departments tab and then the Town Clerks tab. Click "Land Records, Survey and Map Index." Then click "Non-window user." Then click Public Search. Then click Accept. Then you are on the page that allows you to search land records by homeowner name.
- Town of Norwalk (www.norwalkct.org/163/Land.Records). Go to the website. Once there, click "Click here to view land records online." Then click "Non-window user." Then you are on the page that allows you to search land records by property owner name.
- Town of Glastonbury (www.glastonbury-ct.gov). Go to the website. Once there, click Departments. Then click Town Clerk. Then click Land Records. Then click

"Online town clerks records." Then click "Land records indexes." Then click "Web browser user." Then search by name (property owner). Look for tabs labeled Type and Legal. Those tabs will give you the instrument recorded (i.e., deed, judgment lien, tax lien, and so forth) and the property description and/or address.

- Town of Goshen (www.goshenct.gov). Go to the website. Once there, click Government. Then click Town Clerk. Then click the tab on the left labeled "Land records and maps." On the next page, click Kofile, then click "Login as guest." Click "Search public records" on the top tab. Then, on the left side of the page under search type, click Title/Street. Then in the middle, begin searching by name of property owner (last name first), and put in search date (use an older search date to present day). Then click Search at the far top-right side of page. Pay attention to tabs marked Document and Type. Those tabs will give you the instrument recorded (i.e., deed, judgment lien, tax lien, and so forth) and the property description and/or address.

- Town of Salem (www.salemct.gov). Go to the website. Once there, click Departments. Click Town Clerk. Then click Public Records. Then click Website. Then click Land Records. Then click "Non-window users." Then click Public Search. Then click Accept on the disclaimer page. Then start your search based upon the name of the owner of the property. Pay attention to the Type and Legal tabs for what document is recorded and the property address associated with the right property owner you are looking for.

- Town of Voluntown (www.voluntown.gov/land-records/). Go to the website. Click "Public search website." Click "Non-window user" (it's a temperamental tab; sometimes it works and sometimes not).
- Town of Easton (www.eastonct.gov). Go to the website. Once there, click the Government tab. Then click the Town Clerk tab. Then click, on the left side, the "Land records and maps online" tab. The next page is the disclaimer; click Accept. Then click "Guest user web browser." Then click Public Records. On the next page, click Accept Disclaimer. Then you are at a similar page where you are allowed to search the land records via property owner name.
- City of West Hartford (www.westhartfordct.gov). Go to the website. Once there, click the Government tab. Then click the Online Services tab. Then click the Land Records tab. Sign in as a guest, and begin your search by the property owner's last name. Pay attention to the description for the property address you are searching for.

Search by Subscription Only
- Town of Norwich (www.norwichct.org). Go to the website. Once there, click the Government tab. Then click Department. Then click City Records. Then click, on the left side of the page, the tab "Land records subscription needed." Then go to the right side of the page under Quick Links. Download the subscription form, complete, and mail to the office of the town clerk with payment. The form shows where to send payment and the amount it costs. Your choices are one week for $40, one month

for $100, six months for $250, or one year for $400 (this option allows up to five users). I have not acquired access to this site, so I cannot say how the search will go. This is an option if you really want property in Norwich that you see for sale by foreclosure auction. Once you have paid for your subscription, go back to the page where the quick links were, and click "New land records access page" to sign in as a registered user.

- City of Stamford (www.stamfordct.gov). Go to the website. Click Our City and then click Town Clerk. Click Land Records to the left if you did not automatically arrive at that page. Then, at the bottom of the page under Links, click "Application for Access to Stamford Land Records." Then you will be asked a series of questions, and then print the application. Once completed, you have to bring the form to the City and Town Clerks' Office, 888 Washington Boulevard, Stamford, CT 06901 with a check made payable to the City of Stamford for $750. This amount is for a two-year subscription for access to Stamford Land Records online. I have not acquired access personally, so I cannot attest to the ease and comfort of the site. This one is for the aggressive buyers of foreclosure auction properties. Given the fact that the city of Stamford has a growing foreclosure auction market, at least according to the judicial website, this may be something that those who are interested in Stamford properties would find to be a worthy investment.

- Once you have paid for your subscription and are allowed access, go back to links and click "Search land records online" to continue your search. Since I have not signed up for a subscription, I do not know how long it will take to accept application so that you will have access.

As of January 2020, the following towns have no online access to land records. If you find property in any of these towns, you need to visit the town clerk's office in that town and do a physical title rundown or search. Unfortunately, with the exception of Scotland, these towns usually have foreclosure auctions posted on the judicial website.

Lyme (may be part of East Lyme)
New Fairfield
Scotland
Sprague
Shelton
Wallingford

Note: Some websites are not secure, so be wary of putting in any personal information.

LIENS THAT SURVIVE THE FORECLOSURE AUCTION

When there is a foreclosure auction, all liens are extinguished from the property in order to get a clear title transaction—that is, all liens *except* tax liens, sewer liens, water liens, blight liens, and pollution abatement liens. All these liens run with the property, and as such, any successful buyer at the auction would be responsible for payment of those liens. Blight liens and pollution abatement liens are rare but increasing. *Always seek legal counsel for further explanation and advice.*

In addition, IRS liens survive the auction temporarily. If there is an IRS lien on the property, the only way to remove it is by foreclosure auction. However, that lien does not get removed until 120 days after the date the committee deed is recorded upon the land records. *Always seek legal counsel for further explanation and advice.* However, during that 120 days, the IRS has the right to redeem the property, thereby canceling out the successful bidder's title to the property. While I have never seen that happen before, it does not negate the fact that it could.

Another anomaly that sometimes appears on title records is a life-use lien and/or attachment. I am not sure what life use is considered, a lien or attachment or encumbrance. However, I do know that life-use clauses of any property can surely be a deciding factor when looking at a property to purchase at a foreclosure auction. The creation of a life-use clause on a property establishes a stipulation for all further title transactions. Essentially, any life-use encumbrance on a property allows any and all individuals who have a life use of the property, to live in that property for as long as they live, regardless of who maintains title. In addition, you cannot collect any rent from that person and/or persons, nor can you evict them. Sometimes, this is not picked up or noticed in a foreclosure action. Realistically, it is a rarity to see. However, you as the buyer at an auction need to be aware of it. I am not sure if this same stipulation can exist on commercial property. *Always seek legal counsel for further explanation and advice.*

BLIGHT LIENS

This is something new that I am starting to notice on some properties. These liens are taking some buyers by surprise. It is a cause for concern when a purchaser buys a foreclosure auction property and then finds it has a blight lien. At first glance, as a purchaser, you would assume a blight lien gets wiped out along with all other liens, except of course, taxes, sewer, and water liens. However, it has come to my attention that blight liens run with the property. So anyone who purchases a property at a foreclosure auction needs to be aware, if there is a blight lien on the property, then he or she will become responsible for that lien when title transfers to him or her or if a company, whomever it may be. In other words, you as the purchaser will have to pay off the lien in order to further clear your title. This would mostly pose a problem to anyone who is getting a mortgage to purchase the property.

You may be wondering, *What is a blight lien?* I wondered the very same thing. The first time I came across it was a couple of years ago. After researching it on the internet, I found out that blight liens were only legislated sometime around 2012. When a property owner does not take care of his or her property and it becomes an eyesore in the neighborhood, the town or city can fine that property owner. If he or she does not pay the fine, then the town or city slaps a lien on his or her property. In addition, the fine is assessed daily until the repair, damage, and/or dilapidation has been rectified; if not, and it becomes a part of a foreclosure auction, the new owner will assume the lien and the responsibility of making the property acceptable again.

This type of lien on property tends to be located in the lavish market areas of property such as in towns like Westport, Fairfield, Greenwich, Southington, and so forth. In my opinion, it does explain why you might not necessarily see them on property located in the more urban towns and cities such as Bridgeport, Hartford, New Haven, and so forth. These areas are more encumbered by neighborhoods that have such as substantial number of homes in need of repair that it would cost the city a pretty penny to put liens on them. However, it does work to the advantage of those purchasers who want to buy, sell, or rent properties in those less-than-lavish neighborhoods. No blight lien equals less purchase investment money.

ATTEND AUCTION

1. Only bank/certified funds are allowed as deposit to bid; you cannot bring cash or personal checks to bid money. Only bank or certified funds will allow you to bid on the property. The bank or certified funds are made payable to yourself. If you become the successful buyer, the committee will direct you as to whom you endorse the funds over. This is usually the clerk of the superior court.
2. Registration: You will sign the registration sheet with your name, address, and telephone number after you show the committee proof of valid deposit funds.
3. Signing of sales agreement: If you are the successful buyer, you will sign a sales agreement. One copy will go to you, and the other comes back with the committee to be submitted to the court.
4. Individual purchaser: Sign sales agreement as self.
5. Entity purchaser: Sign sales agreement as the authorized agent of entity, assuming this is acceptable to the committee. If you are attempting to purchase property in a company name, contact the committee beforehand to make sure it's OK.
6. Cannot sign as power of attorney: You cannot purchase property as power of attorney for someone else.
7. Endorsing check (clerk of the Superior Court): See subsection 1 above.

CLOSE WITH COURT-APPOINTED COMMITTEE

1. Buyer—mortgage transaction: Need your own attorney.
2. Buyer—cash transaction: Can close on your own with court-appointed committee or if more comfortable, with your own attorney.
3. Certified/bank funds only payable to clerk of Superior Court: Final funds due can only be certified or bank funds.
4. Committee deed: At the closing you as the buyer get a committee deed (this document transfers the title into your name), which you must record immediately upon the respective land records.
5. Conveyance tax return: You will get a conveyance tax return that has to be recorded, but please be aware there is no conveyance tax due, and court-appointed foreclosure auction transactions are tax exempt.

WHAT TO DO AFTER TITLE PASSES/ PROBLEMS THAT MAY ARISE

1. Record the committee deed the same day of closing, if possible.
2. Tenants in property: Tenants are a concern because you as the buyer are responsible for removing them from the property if you do not want them there. Always find out if there are tenants in the property prior to moving full steam ahead with purchasing a property at a foreclosure auction. If you are okay with it, no problem. But if not, you will be responsible for the following: ejectment or eviction, which can add to your cost in the purchase of this property. *Always seek out legal counsel if it comes to having to do this.*
3. Tenants and/or owners living in the property will have the option of filing a stay of execution, which means he or she can petition the court for more time to stay in the property in order to find other housing. The decision is left up to the court, *but* most of the time, petition is granted.

EXCEPTIONS TO A SUCCESSFUL FORECLOSURE AUCTION SALE/ REASONS WHY SALE IS CANCELED

In your search for the purchase of a foreclosure auction property, the sale may be canceled. If it is, the following are the most popular reasons why:

1. Bankruptcy (defendant action): If the defendant files bankruptcy, then the sale will be canceled. Sometimes, it will come up again, but sometimes it will not. It depends on the chapter filed (i.e., 7 or 13 or 11). From what I gather, chapter 7 tends to lead to a new sale order, so there would be hope for those of you who really want a particular property. If 13 is filed, then it's most likely not going to be available again since this allows the property owner to pay off past-due debt in a plan over five years, allowing the property owner the right to keep the property. I am not sure about chapter 11 since I am very unfamiliar with it. In all cases, please seek out legal counsel for confirmation.

2. Forbearance/modification (defendant/plaintiff action): If a property owner and the entity bringing the lawsuit come to an agreement or payment arrangement and they enter into a forbearance or modification agreement, then the lawsuit gets vacated or withdrawn.

3. Payoff (defendant/plaintiff action): If a property owner pays off the entirety of the past-due amounts, then the lawsuit gets vacated or withdrawn.

BONUS

For those enthusiasts who really want to get into it, there are other properties you can purchase via sale (see chapter 5).

CHAPTER 5

MUNICIPAL TAX DEED SALES

These are a different breed of capturing auction properties. These are not sales by virtue of a foreclosure lawsuit. Simply put, for anyone who owes taxes, sewer, and/or water and has not paid, the town or city has a right to offer the debt up for sale to the public at an auction in exchange for the title to the property. A notice is issued to the homeowner and lien holders on the property, and that notice is listed in the newspaper and/or on a website to the public. The notice states that if those debts are not satisfied, the property is to be offered for sale at an auction on a given date.

    This is a notice that goes out to the property owner. Should no one respond, the auction occurs. Then whoever purchases it gets the property free and clear of all liens, with few exceptions, after six months has passed.

    This information is reflective of a website that I found to be very helpful with these kinds of sales, which not only explains the process but also lists the sales they have. I did notice that the properties via this website have a listing with more commercial lots, and these listings appear mostly in the upper part of the state of Connecticut. The website is www.cttaxsales.com.

This website is very informative about the process; it's the best I have seen. It has a tab for general information about how the tax sale process works, which I recommend. It has a listing of current municipal tax deed sales, but you must be very aggressive in following up on them so you do not miss the opportunity. As I said, the sales are not offered every week like foreclosure auctions and are grouped and sold by the town or city on a chosen date.

You still have to do all your homework to gain knowledge of a particular piece of property, but it's a different way to obtain property. And if for some reason the property owner or another lien holder wants to pay off the debt prior to the expiration of the six months, you will get your money back plus interest. Either way, you make some money if you have the time and money to make some investments.

There is one matter regarding money with these transactions that I would like to lift up. Because these properties are sold in groups, you should be aware that there is a $5,000 deposit per property you are interested in purchasing. At least, this is true of this website.

These sales are not for the fainthearted but are for those who have substantial funding to put up at once. These sales offer an opportunity to purchase multiple pieces at one time. However, this is a great opportunity for the one-home shopper or the multiple-piece investor.

Municipal tax deed sales are not lawsuits but are like foreclosure sale auction with a few exceptions. These exceptions are particular to the website above only.

Note: Some websites are not secure, so be wary of putting in any personal information.

Now that you know where you can find all about a foreclosure auction property you would like to purchase, you are prepared to attend a sale and make that purchase.

Here is where I leave you. I hope that you all enjoy your journey of purchasing foreclosure auction and/or tax deed sale properties in Connecticut. I hope I have rendered you with enough substantial information and knowledge that will make this process easier for you.

Remember, *this book does not represent legal advice, and you should seek legal counsel for further explanation* of anything you read here in this book, or on any website to which you are referred.

I am open to all questions regarding my book. I will be holding and/or teaching classes soon for those who would like a chance to hear my views verbally and get a hands-on lesson about the contents herein. You can contact me for further details.

My contact information is:
Sonya Green
srcparalegalservicesllc@gmail.com
203-218-1723